My
Sea Eagle
Odyssey

My Sea Eagle Odyssey

A Wildlife Artist's Quest to paint White-tailed Eagles

R Leonard Hollands

Lamorna Publications

Lamorna Publications

Yew Tree Studio, Marshwood, Bridport,
Dorset DT6 5QF   01297 678566

First published in 2008
This edition published 2021

© R Leonard Hollands 2008 and 2021

Set in 12pt Verdana

ISBN 978-0-9933898-4-9

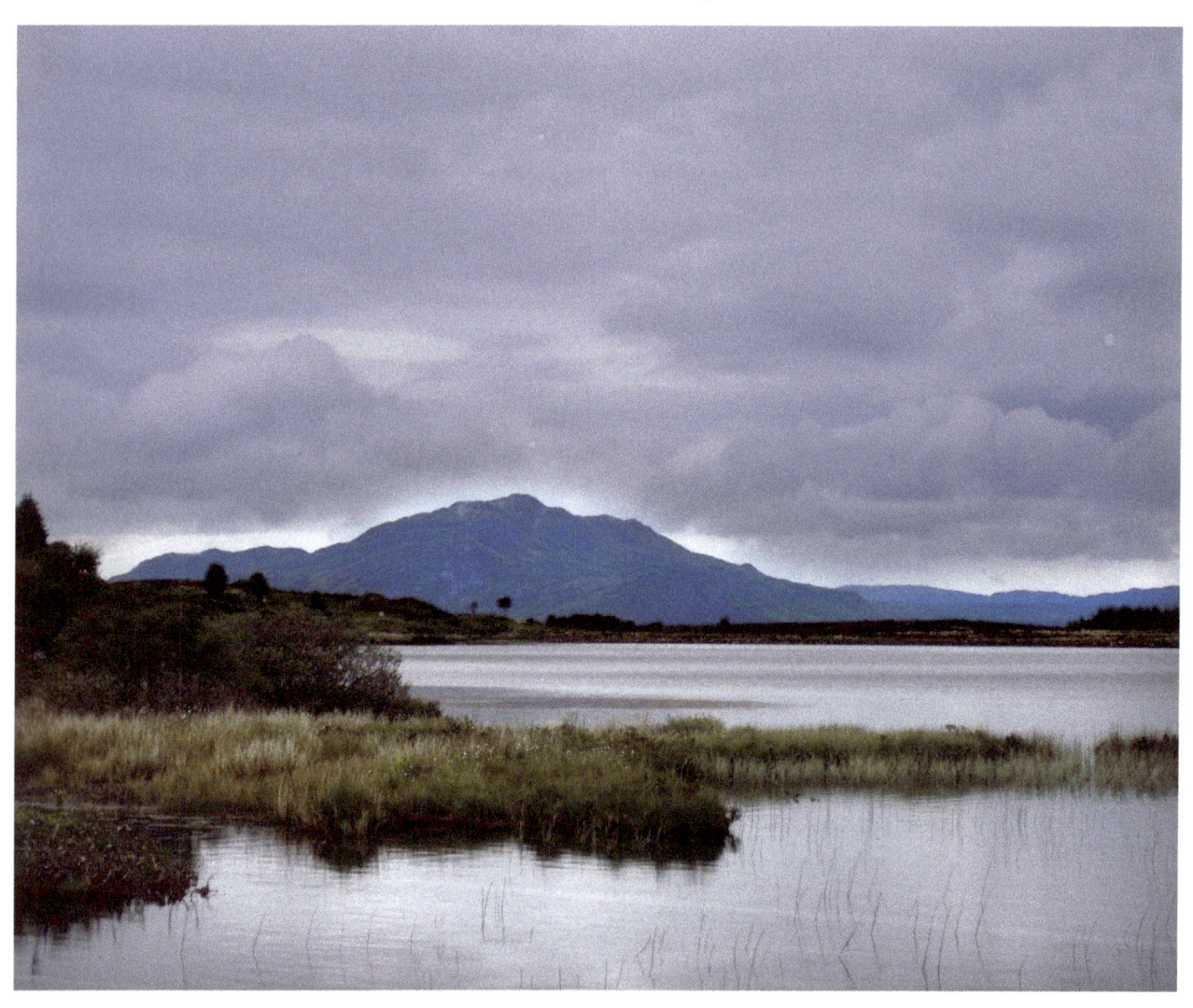

Mull – My Destination

Contents

This book is dedicated to my wife, Trish, who supported me in this venture and endured the hardships as well as sharing the rewards of my Odyssey.

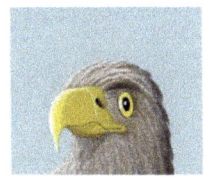

Preparations

I have not travelled as widely as many wildlife artists specifically to find a subject. I am usually content to sketch in the field whatever I happen to see wherever I happen to be, then making finished paintings from some of them back in the studio. But there have been some exceptions, and a notable one was my desire, in 2007, to paint the magnificent White-tailed Eagle, or Sea Eagle as it is widely and affectionately known. I live in West Dorset so this was not going to be a one day exercise as my quarry can best be seen on the Hebridean Isle of Mull.

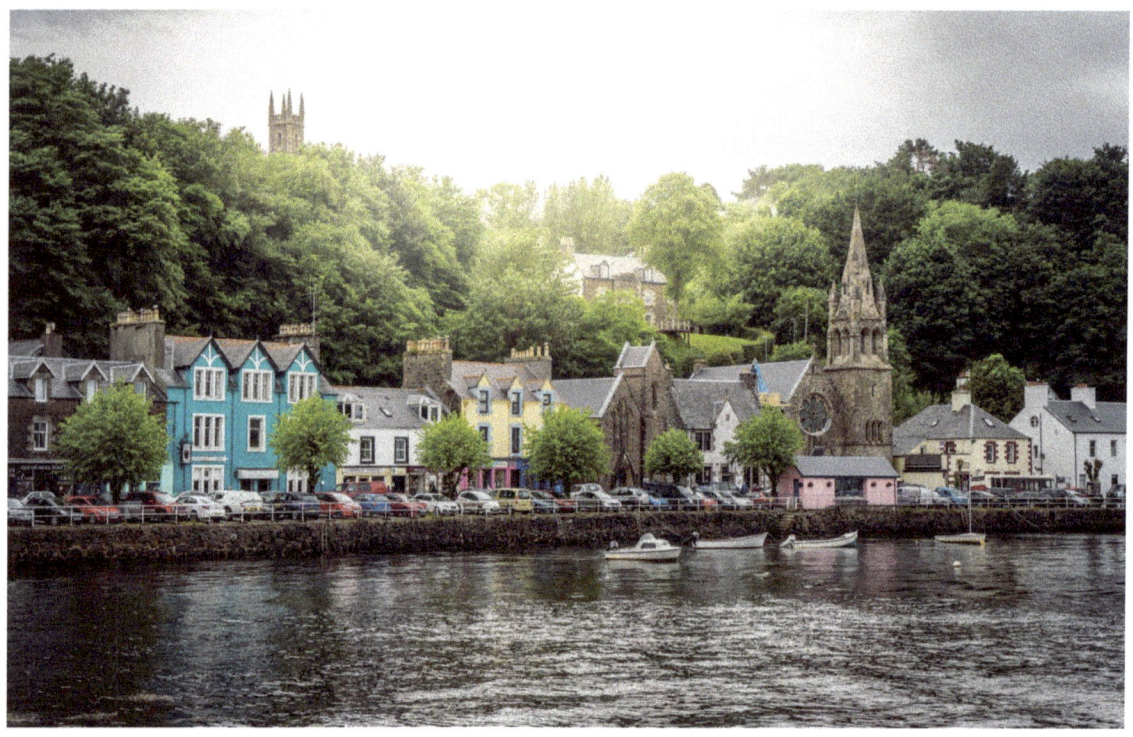

Tobermory, Mull

My first step was to make contact with RSPB Scotland's Mull Officer, David Sexton, to discuss how my aim might be achieved since I clearly would not be able to get the field sketches I would need in one short visit to a crowded hide. (The public, by appointment, visit the hide for a couple of set periods each day.) I am greatly indebted to David and his team for the help and cooperation I received, even including excellent advice on accommodation on Mull, which was duly booked on the basis of "as near as possible to the nest site!"

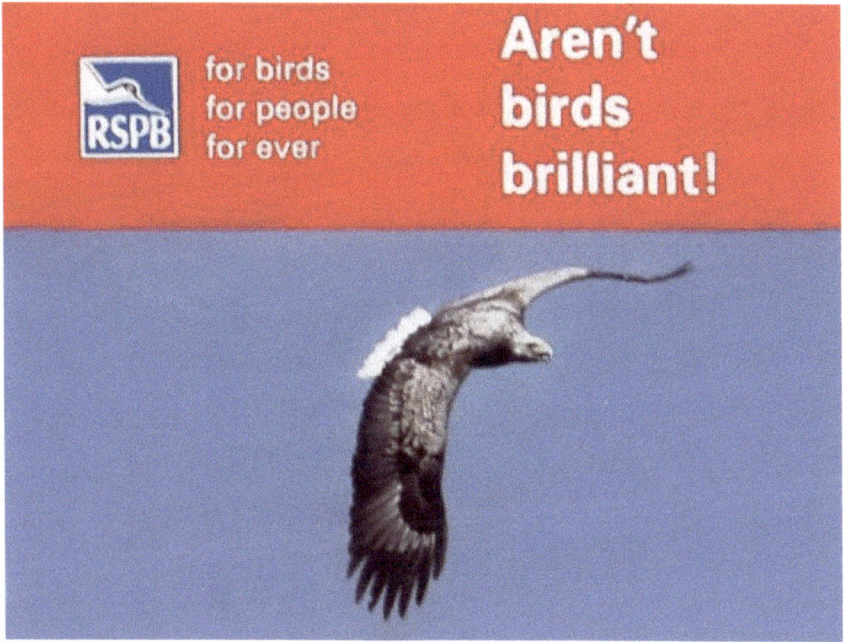

Having planned all this in detail months in advance, I then had to wait as patiently as I could for the time to come round. Of course, in the end it came all too fast and I had my usual scrabble to find the right sketch books, OS maps, and much more that I could have done earlier.

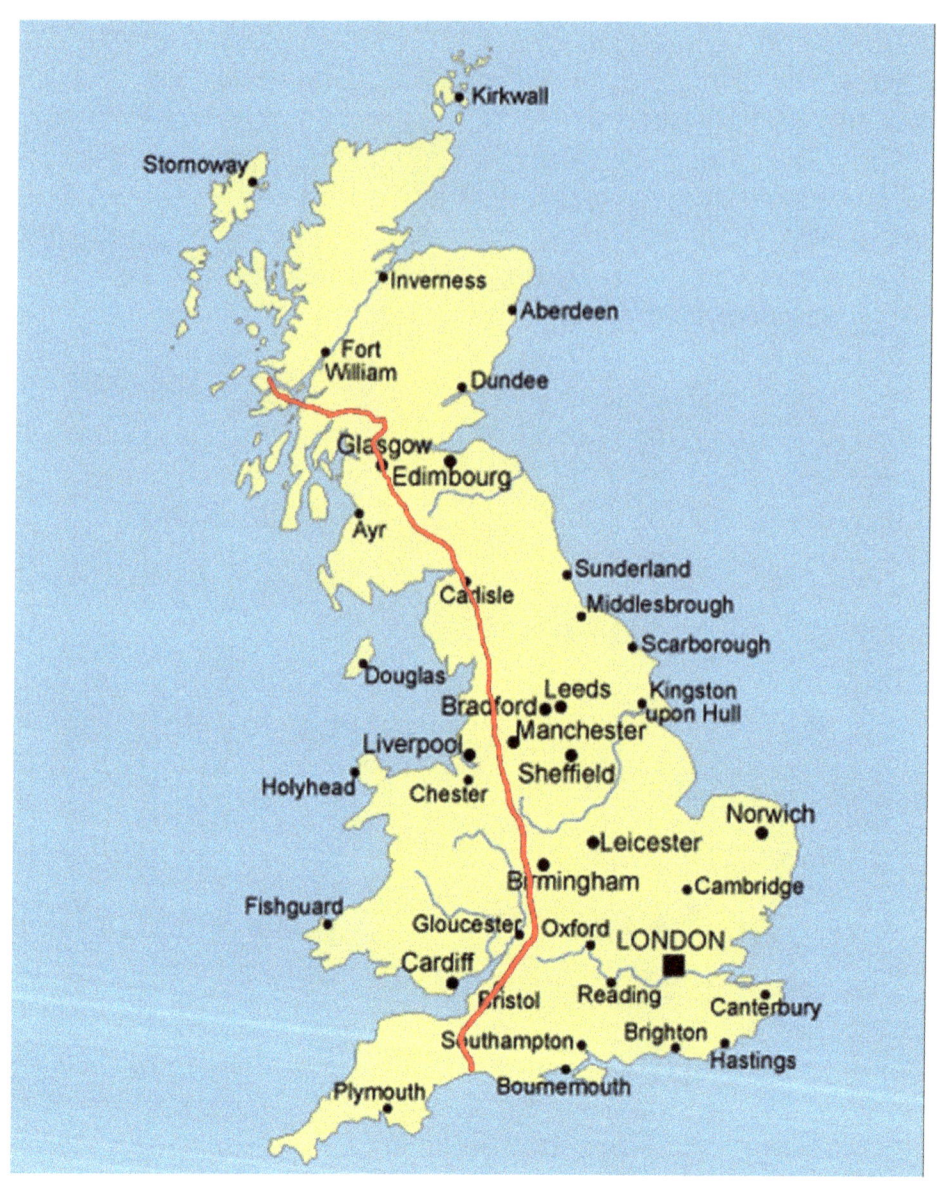

The Journey

The Journey

At last the day came, and we set off on the long journey north with optics and sketch books etc piled up in the car.

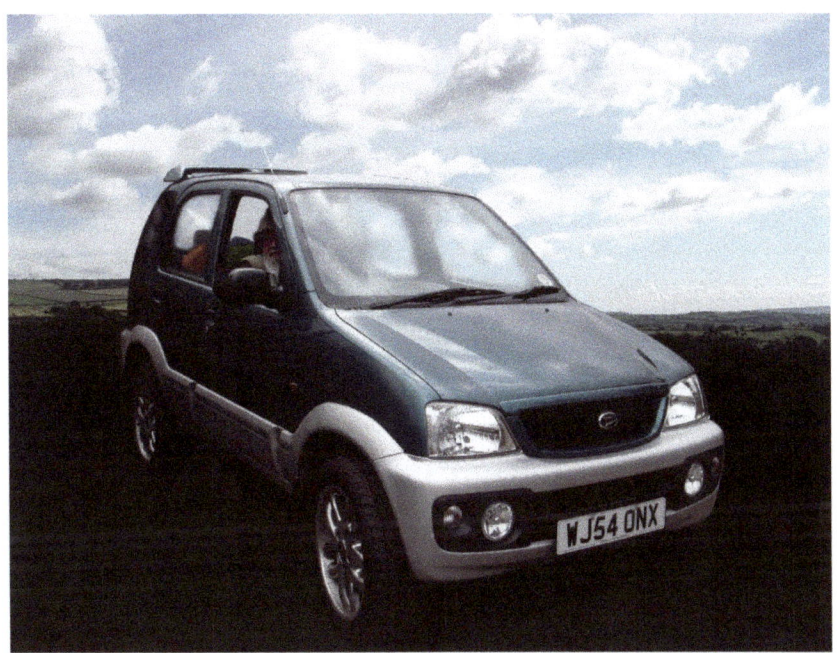

We stopped overnight at Luss on the banks of Loch Lomond which gave me some sketching opportunities including a female merganser and a female goosander in close proximity to each other affording a perfect opportunity to compare them.

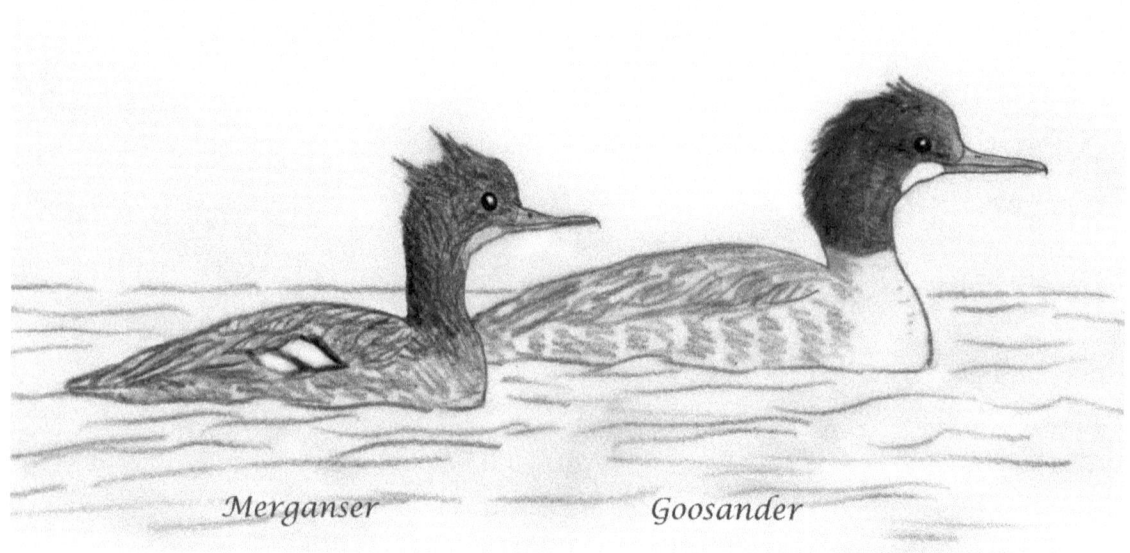

Merganser   *Goosander*

As we continued our journey the next day the weather was good and we enjoyed the superb scenery......until just before Oban. Then the rain, which was to become so familiar, started and the views disappeared. Consequently, on the ferry from Oban over to Mull I got rather wet out on deck sketching auks, gannets and shearwaters, but I don't like to miss opportunities, especially when there are birds around which I don't get to see at home.

I was later inspired to add some manx shearwaters to one of my seascape paintings.

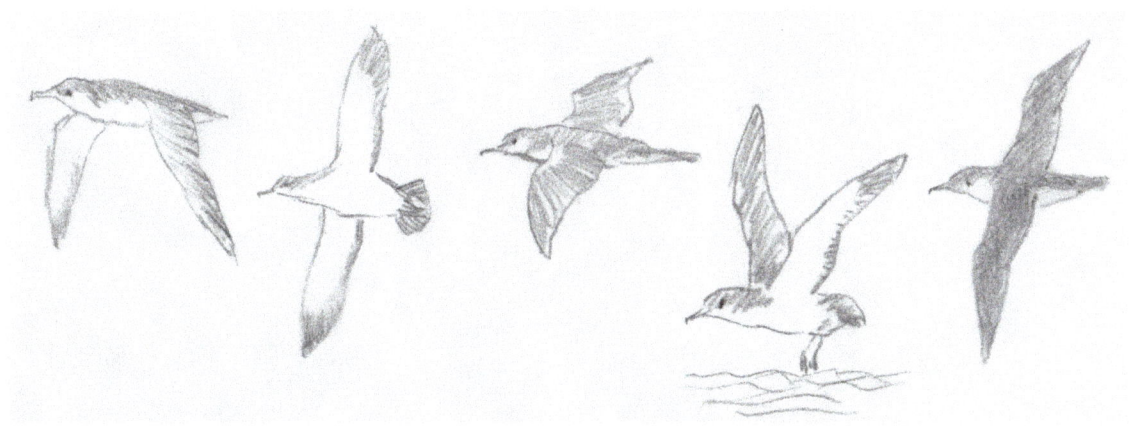

Wet and Windy Sketching

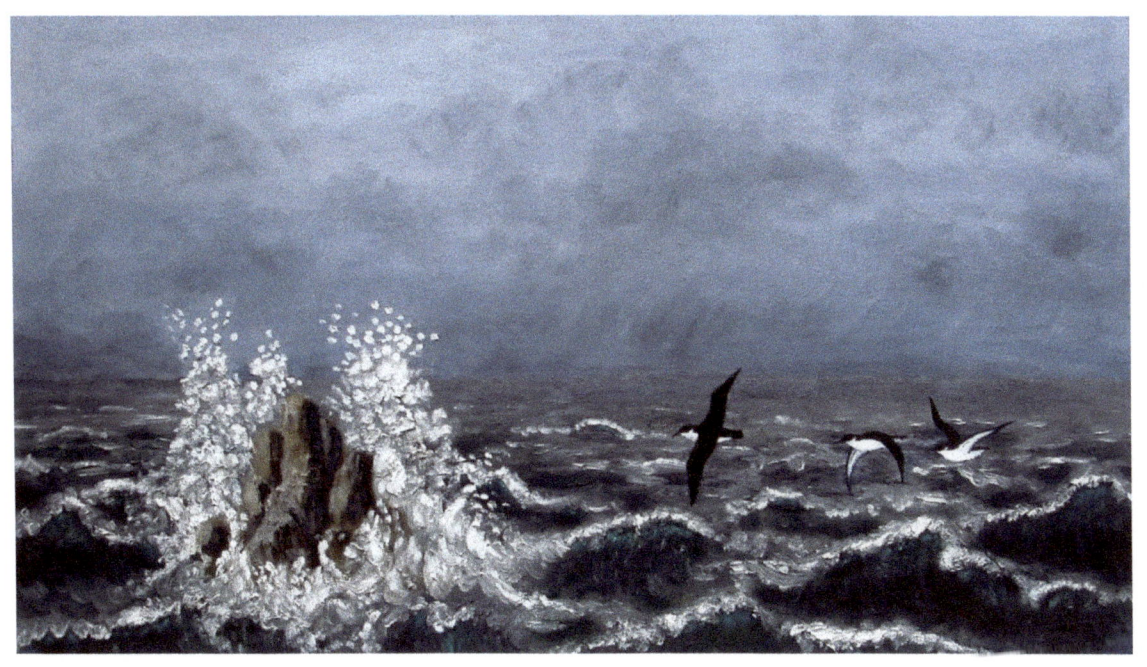

Stormy Sea with Manx Shearwaters

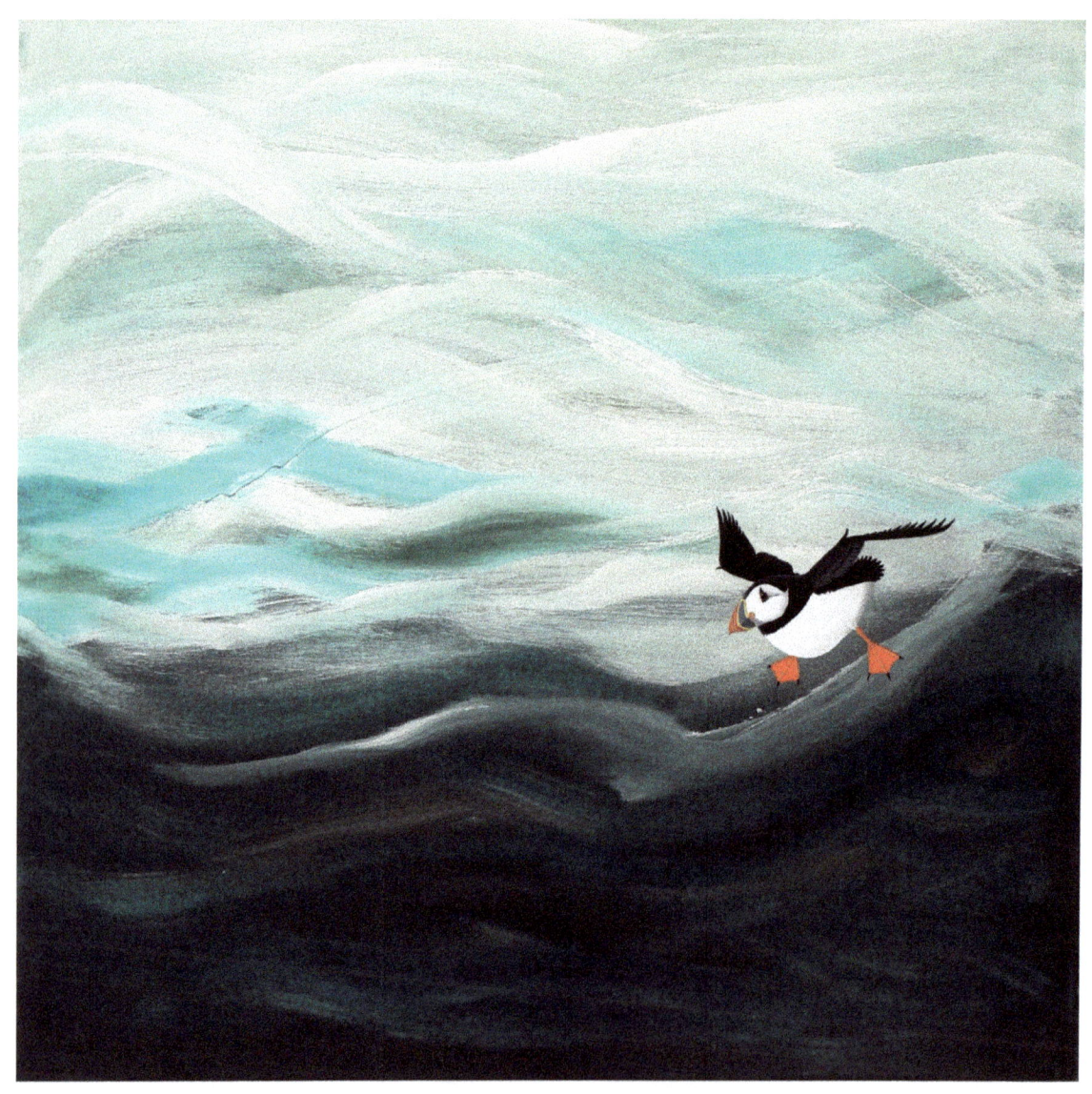

Dancing with the Waves

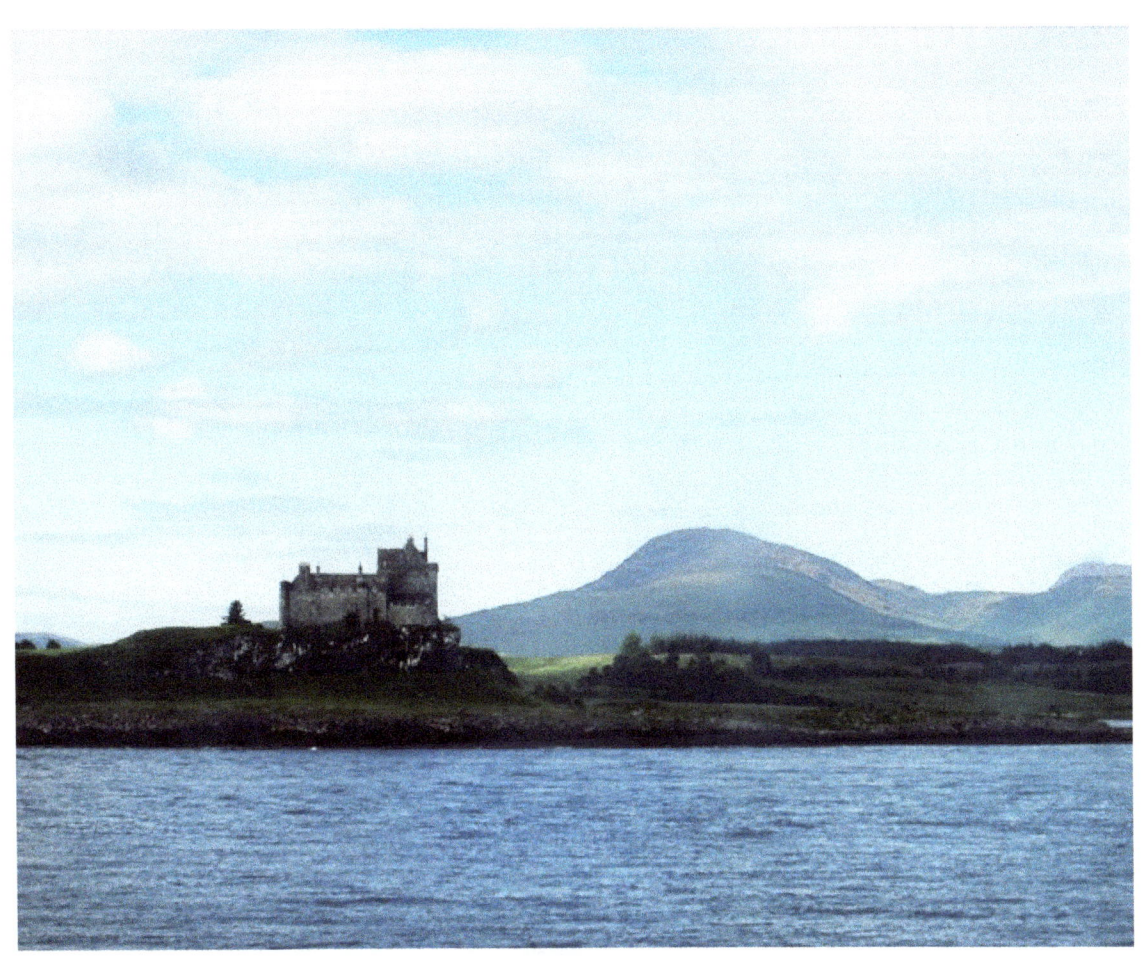

Mull approach

Arrival on Mull

Our arrival on Mull, then, was a wet one, but the bed and breakfast accommodation was welcoming, *and* the owner, Debbie McFadden, turned out herself to be no mean wildlife artist so I felt very much at home. The following morning I met up (you've guessed it – in the rain!) with David Sexton who took me to the Sea Eagles' eyrie on Loch Frisa and briefed me on access, how close I was allowed to get, etc, as the welfare of these majestic birds is of paramount importance.

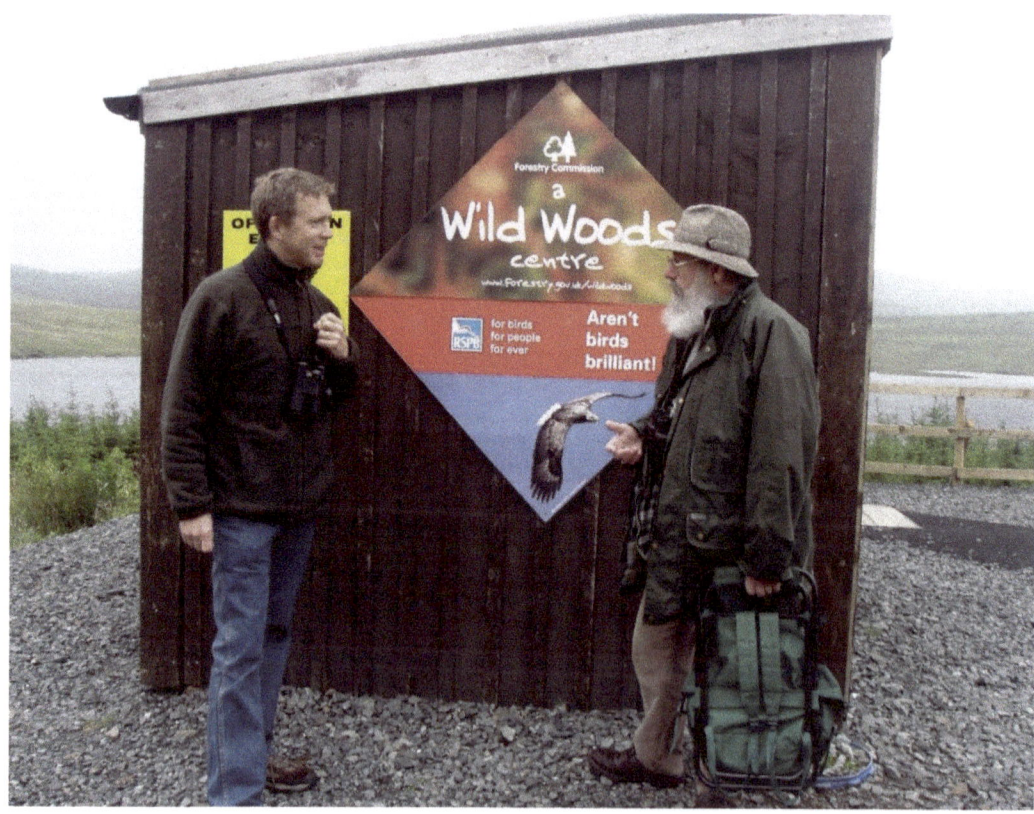

I had chosen to make my odyssey in June when the young were virtually fully grown. The huge size of White-tailed Eagles and the high powered scope I was using meant that I could manage adequately at the permitted viewing distance.

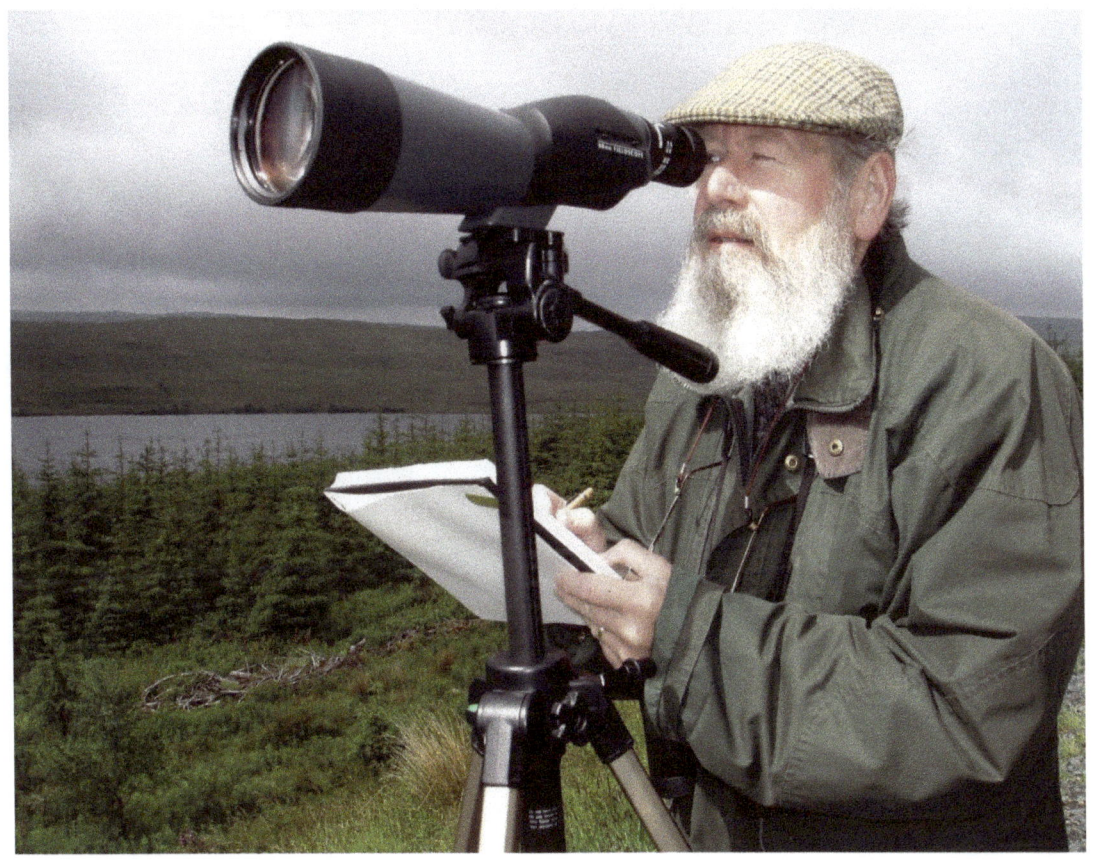

Getting the measure

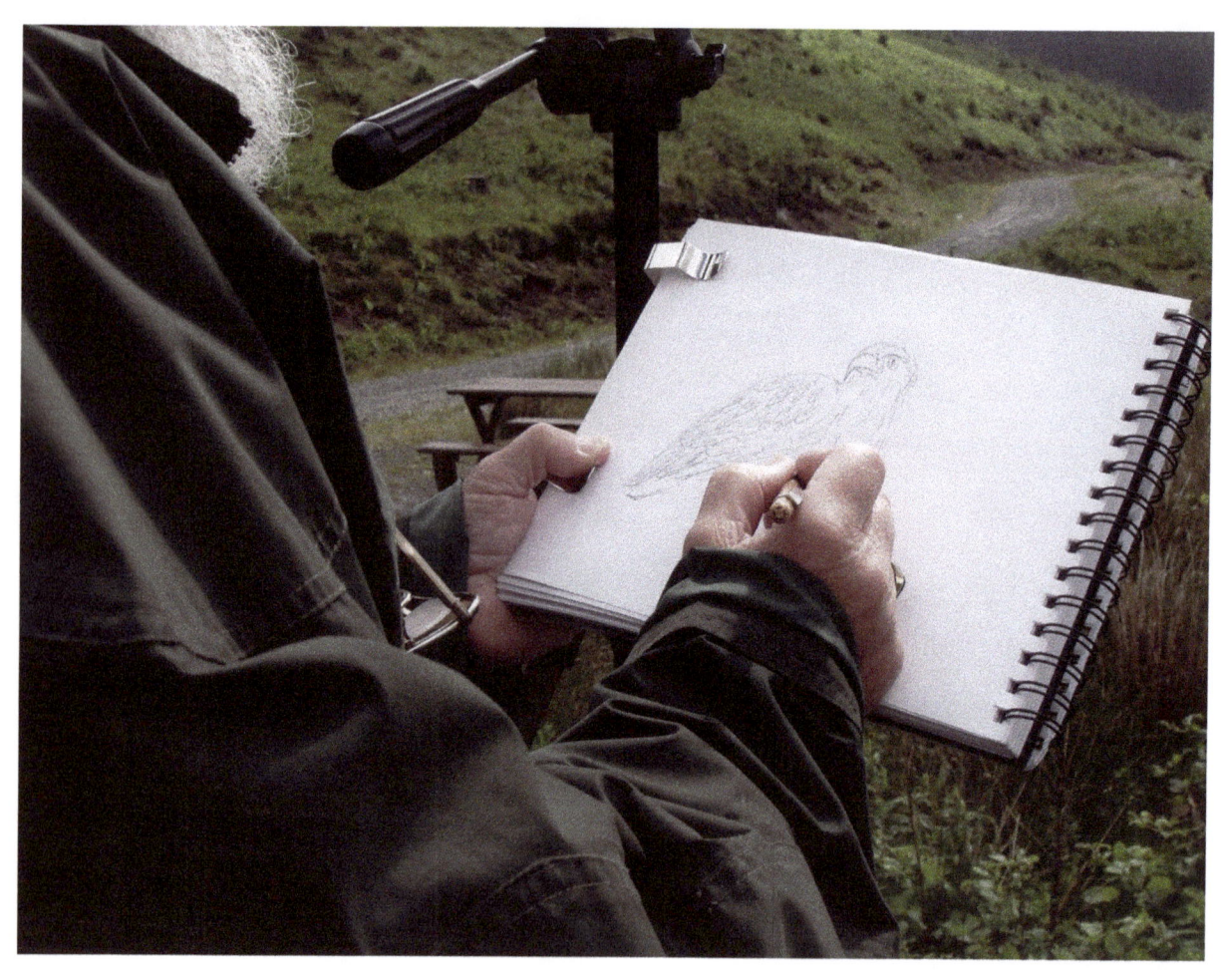

Work begins in earnest

Sketching Begins

On my first visit the mother bird made an appearance, just as the rain backed off for a few minutes and I was able to make my first rapid sketches without the sketchbook becoming waterlogged. Having set up the routine, over the next few days I tried to get to the nest site each time there was a slight lull in the *almost* incessant rain. Gradually I built up a good body of rough sketches from which I felt confident I could produce a painting or two back in my studio.

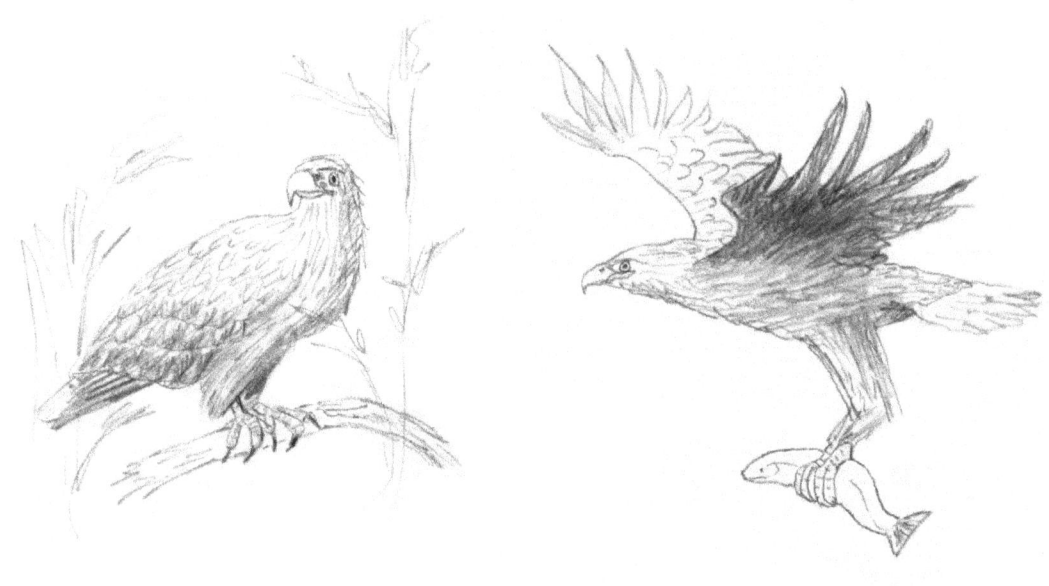

Initial 'roughs'

I was thrilled to get some really close views of the adults flying to and from the nest past my vantage point, enabling me to refine some of my rough sketches.

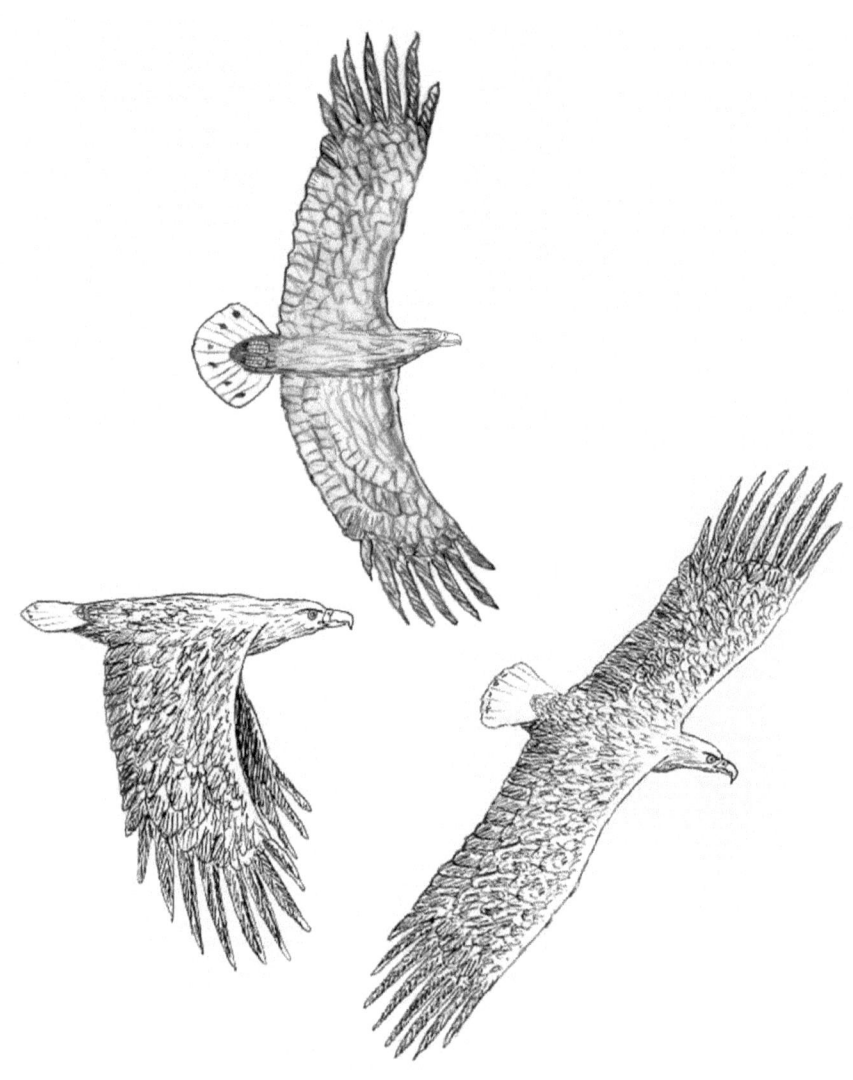

Sympathy for the Sea Eagle

One morning I arrived at about 5.30 and found the father Sea Eagle sitting in a tree looking absolutely soaked and bedraggled. He had his shoulders deeply hunched against the rain and looked as if he had sat like that all night, and most dejected he looked too. I felt so sorry for him. He could hardly be bothered to react at all beyond the occasional swivel of his shaggy head when first one, then two, and finally four common gulls – they nest on the other side of the loch – relentlessly mobbed him. He remained unmoved and his cheeky, and tiny by comparison, would-be assailants eventually gave up. I watched this from inside the car as the rain continued to lash down, and made this sketch of the sorry scene. When I left just before 8 to go back for my breakfast the Sea Eagle still hadn't moved.

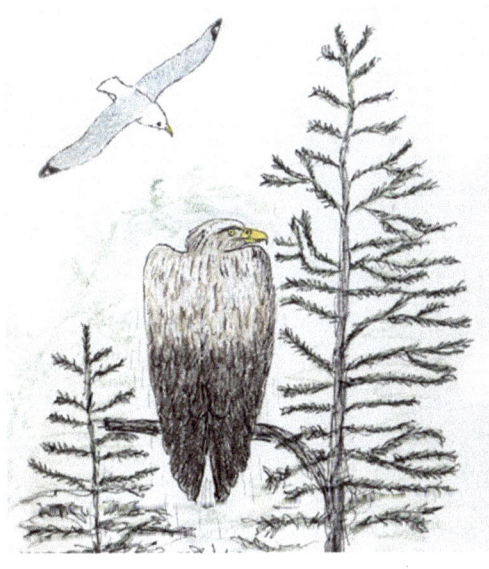

Iona

Before our stay on Mull was over, I was anxious to take the opportunity to cross the short sea strait to visit the tiny island of Iona. Having an interest in Celtic spirituality, I was desirous to see the place where Saint Columba landed and established the monastery which became the centre from which the Celtic Church spread out across our Land.

On the drive to Fionphort to take the little ferry across to Iona, we took the opportunity to visit the beautiful Calgary Bay where some sketching was obligatory.

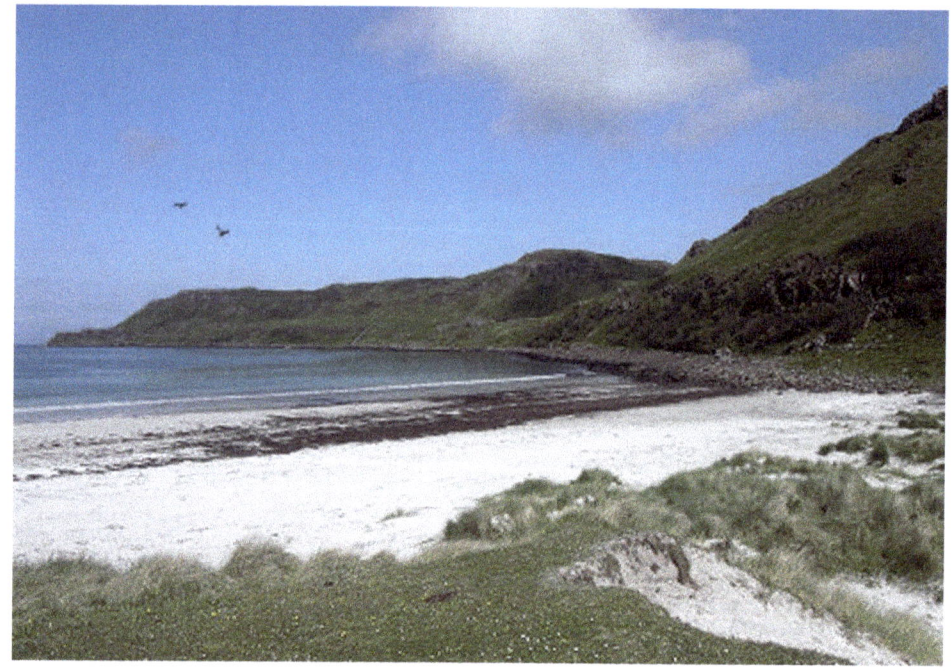

Calgary Bay

Once on Iona we looked at the present Abbey building, old, but much later than the original Celtic foundation, of course, and then set out in earnest to find Iona's special bird – the corncrake. The place was alive with them, their rasping call sounding on every side. But could we spot one? NO. They are shorter than the grass they inhabit and, for all their noise, are very secretive. We met a lady who said she had lived in the middle of them for many years but had never seen one!

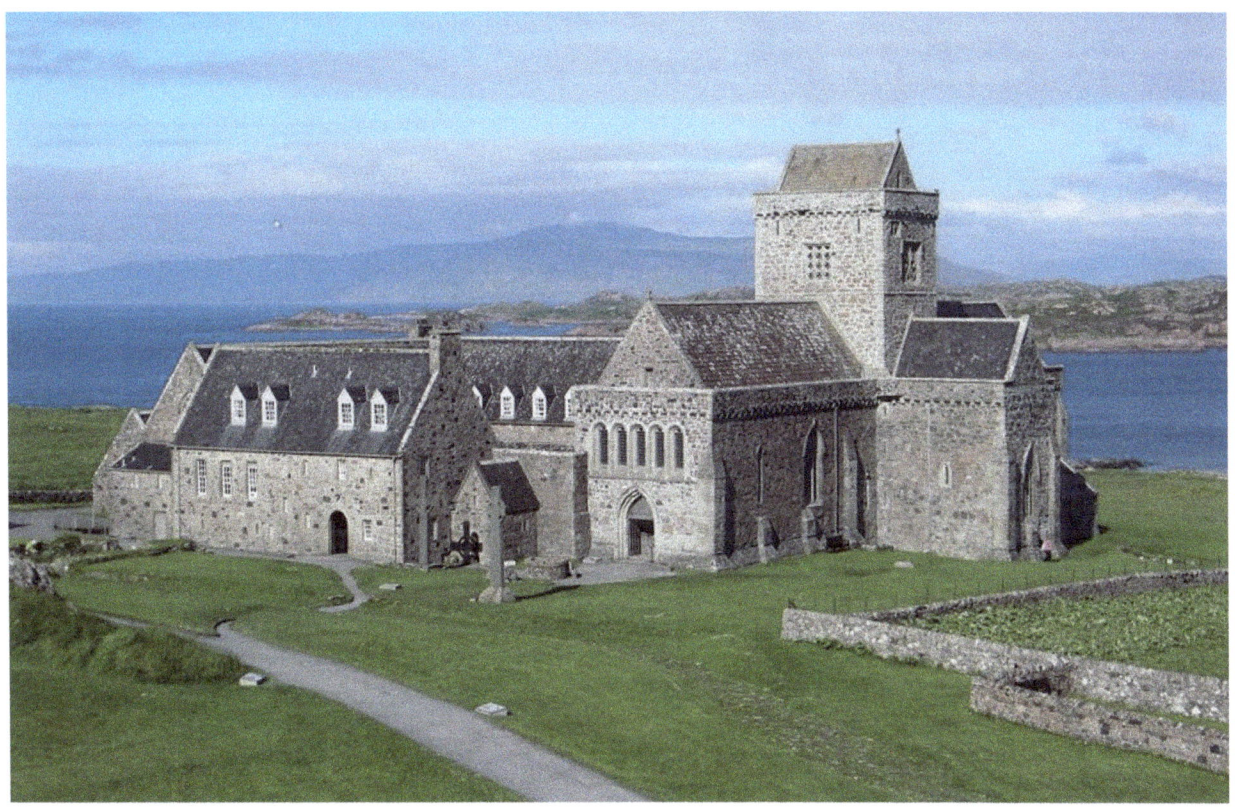

Iona Abbey

It was only a slight disappointment not to see one as it was so impressive to be surrounded by such an abundance of their grating calls – a bit like running one's finger across the teeth of a comb. I had managed to see corncrakes in the past much farther South, but the best view I ever had of one was on the Isle of Islay. From the seclusion of its grass habitat it suddenly hopped up into full view atop a low stone wall! One has occasional strokes of luck like that to offset the hours spent in failure!

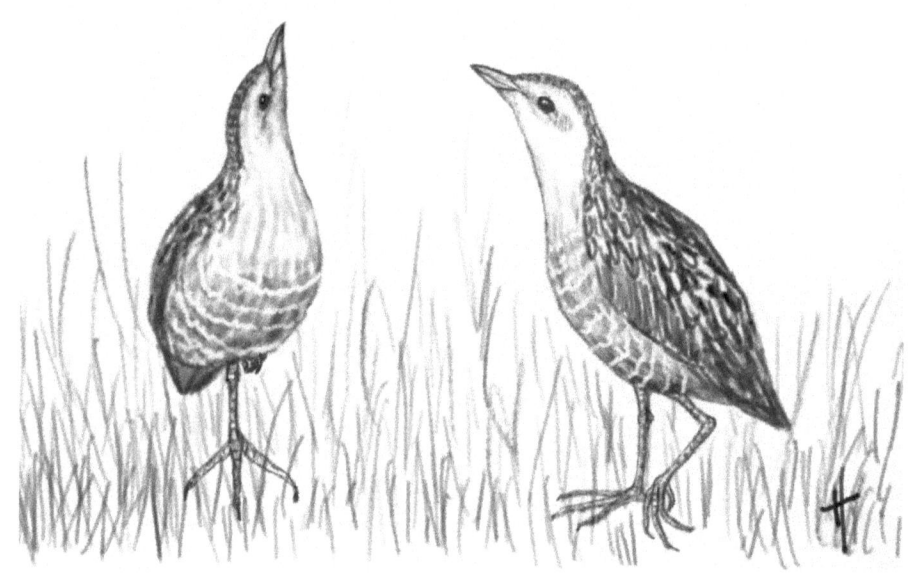

Corncrakes

Dry at last...but too late!

On the morning we left Mull the sun came out and from the retreating ferry we looked back and saw just how beautiful the island is when *not* shrouded in mist and cloud. I decided I must return some time just to see the scenery......not that I wouldn't want to have another chance to watch the Sea Eagles again; of course I would! And I only know one way to watch and that's with a sketchbook in hand.

I had decided that if we were going as far as Scotland we would also fit in a visit to Islay, a favourite island of mine. The weather here remained fine and in a couple of days I had sketched fulmars, black guillemots, choughs, hares and more. And we witnessed the most *incredible* sunsets at around eleven o'clock at night!

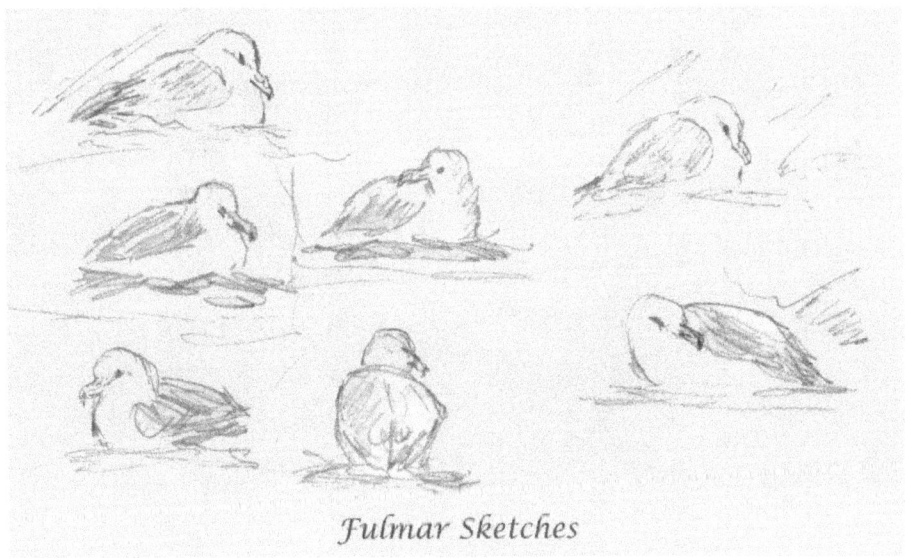

Fulmar Sketches

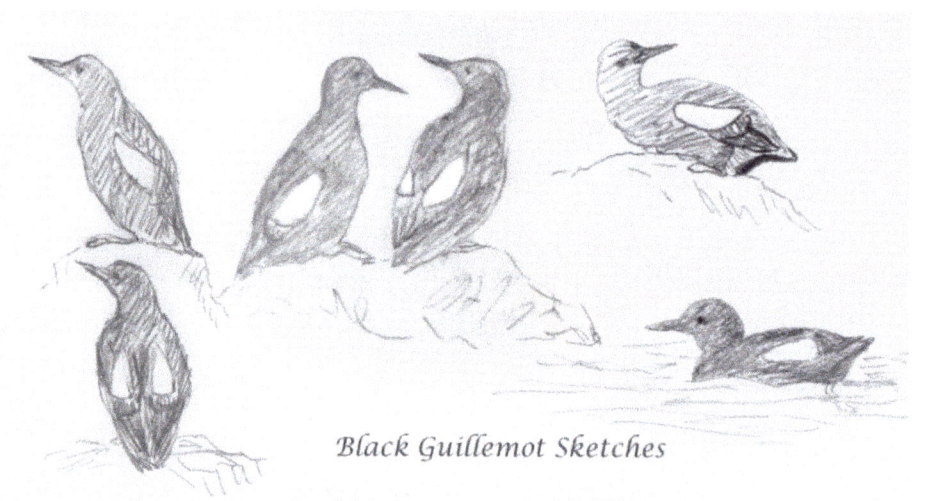

Black Guillemot Sketches

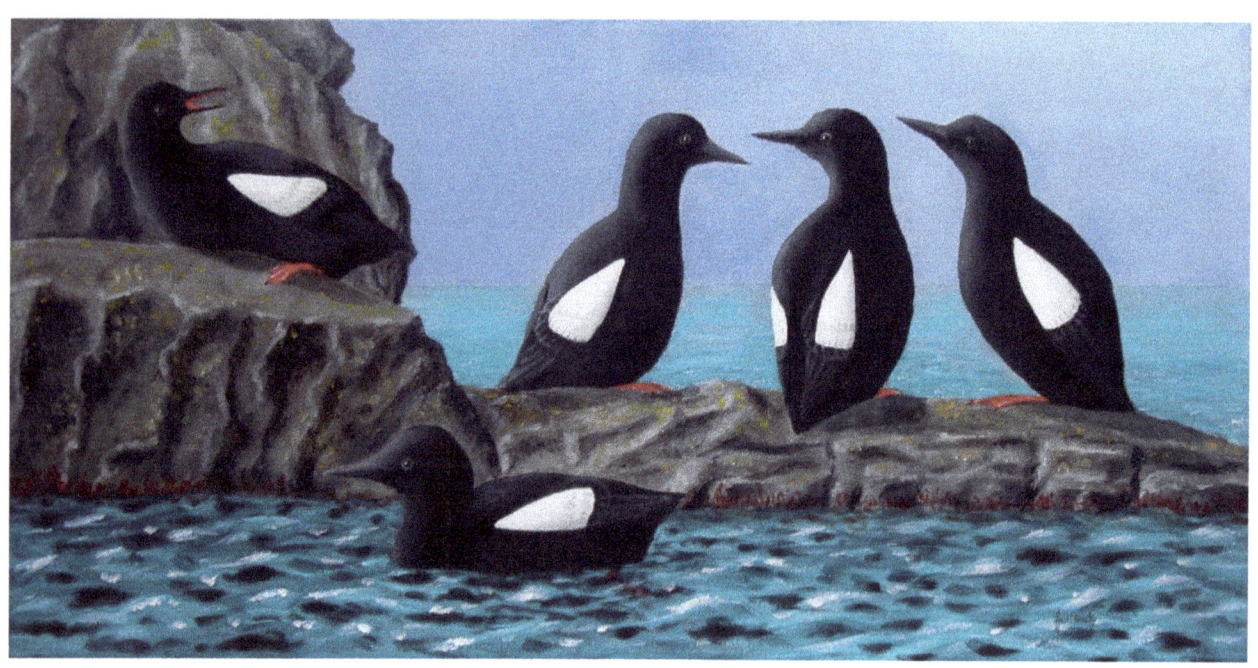

Black Guilemots

19

Some four years later the recollection of the Islay hares and those fantastic evening skies inspired this evocation.

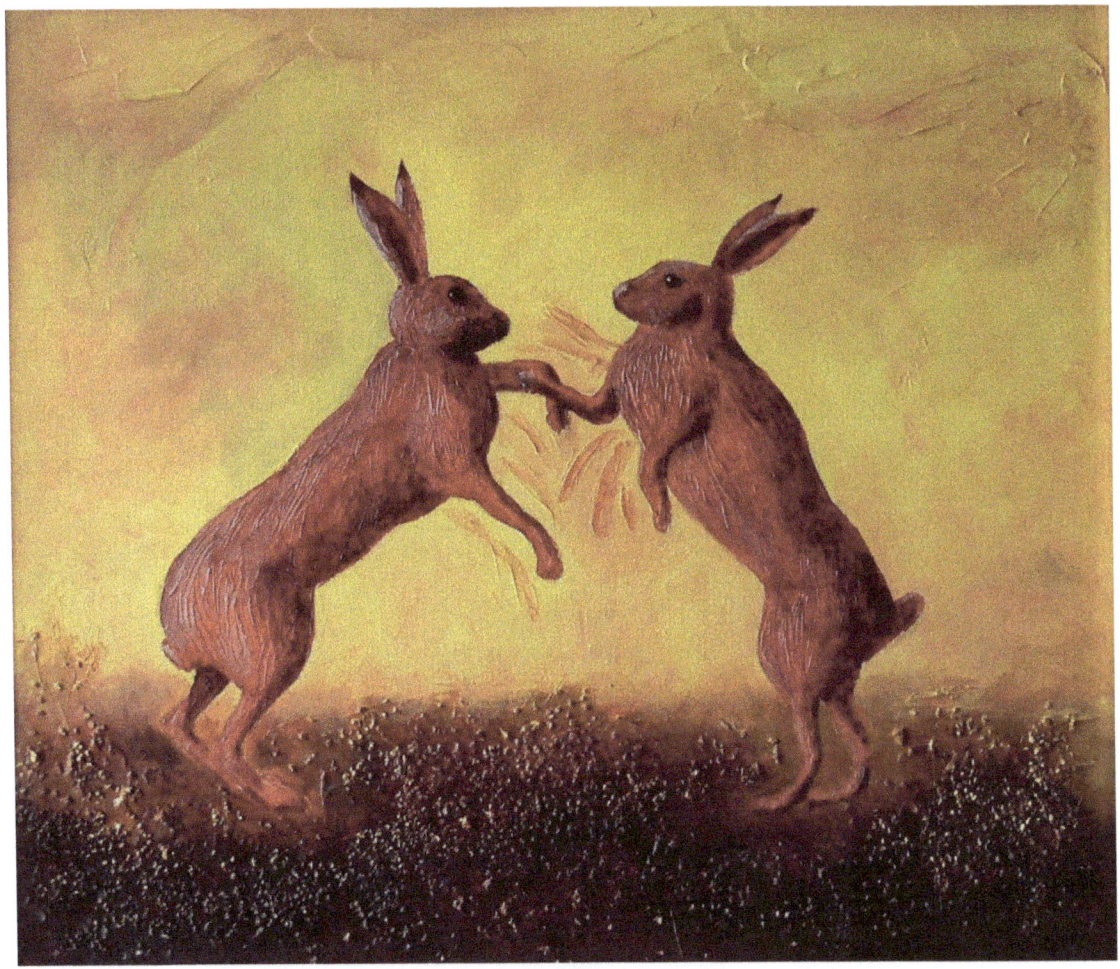

Fisticuffs at Sunset

But to return to 2007. We said farewell to Islay and made our way back to Dorset.

And Finally….

Before starting on my Sea Eagle paintings I still had one more thing to do. I arranged to visit the Natural History Museum at Tring to examine the plumage in detail. The important thing about *field* sketches is to get the *characteristics* of the subject; its "jizz" – typical or, for that matter, *unusual* poses, the shape of the bird and its behaviour, etc. These will inform the 'life' of the painting. But it is not always possible to get all the finer details of the plumage, and the way the feathers lie, and so on in the field. Close up and personal is required to ensure an accurate portrayal of the subject.

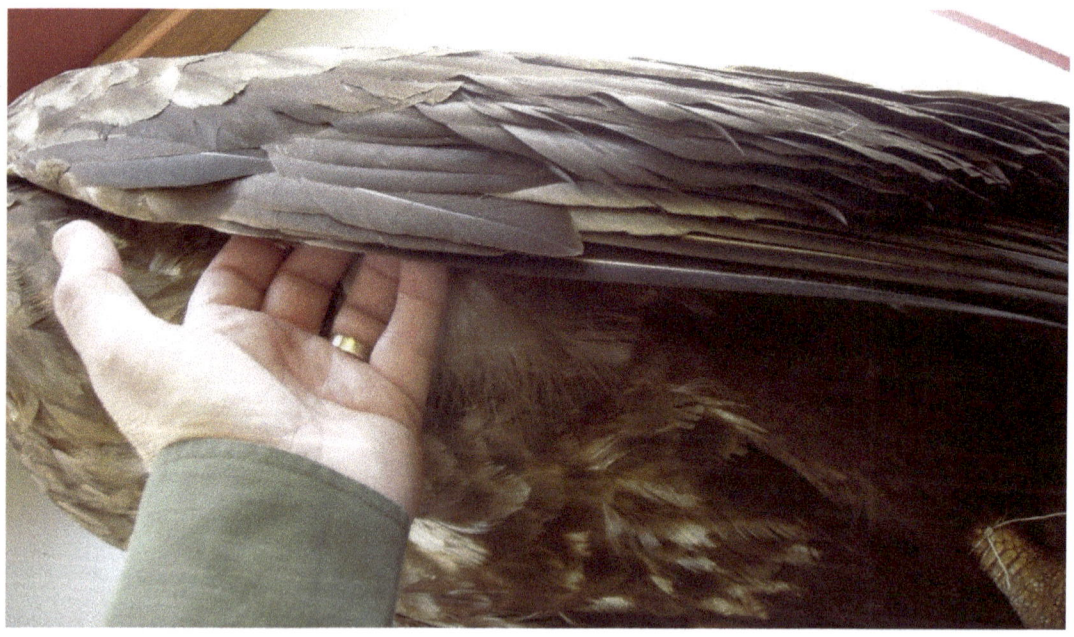

My close encounter with a Sea Eagle

I was met at Tring by the curator, Katrina Cook, who was most helpful and provided me with "skins," not only of the White-tailed Eagle, but also several other birds on which I was then working.

And another coincidence, Katrina, as well as being curator, is *also* a wildlife artist, and an extremely talented one too.

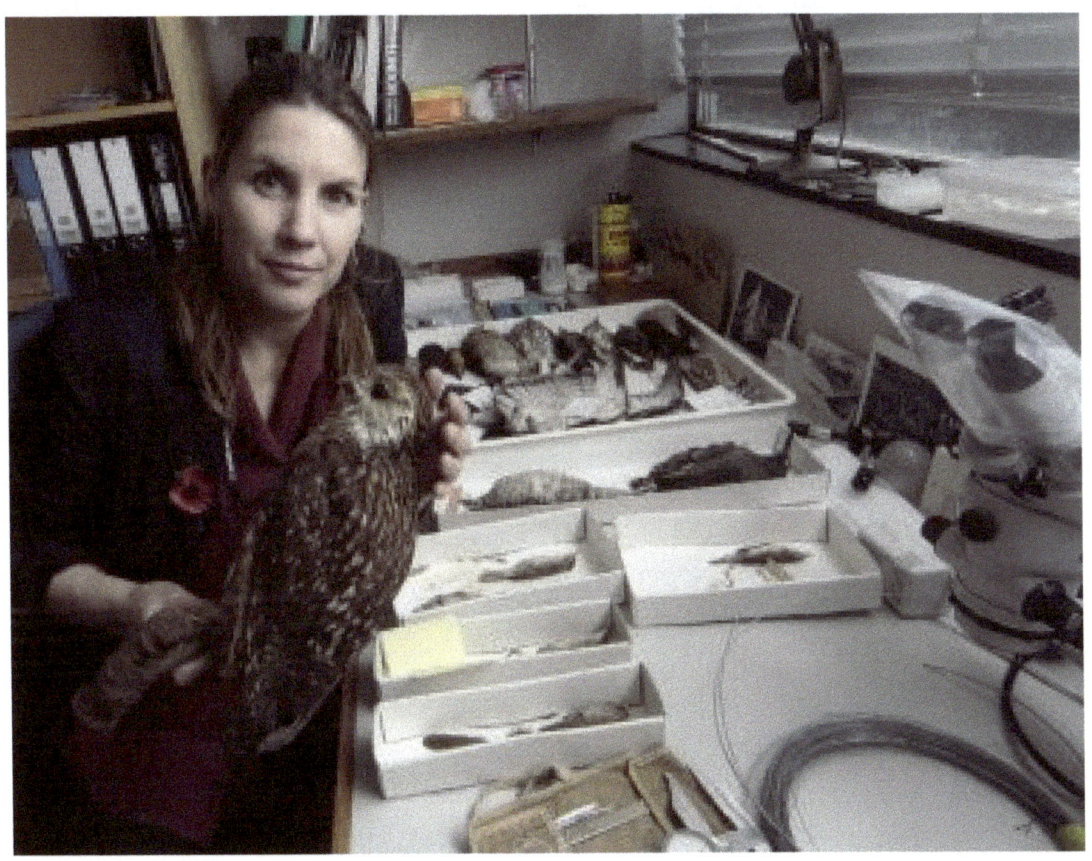

And so I was finally able to set to work in the studio and, over the following months produced two paintings, one of the Sea Eagle in flight with a semi-abstract sea/sky background, and one of a perched bird with its mate flying overhead. In the latter I have 'suggested' the Loch Frisa setting but used artist's licence to move the trees around to get a clear view of the bird's favourite perch.

In these paintings I have painted the backgrounds in acrylics and the birds themselves in oils. I also made an alternative version of the eagle in flight using digital 'magic.' For me they make a satisfactory conclusion to my Sea Eagle Odyssey – my yearning to find and 'capture' these majestic creatures.

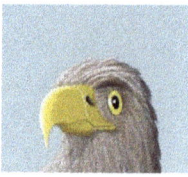

The Paintings

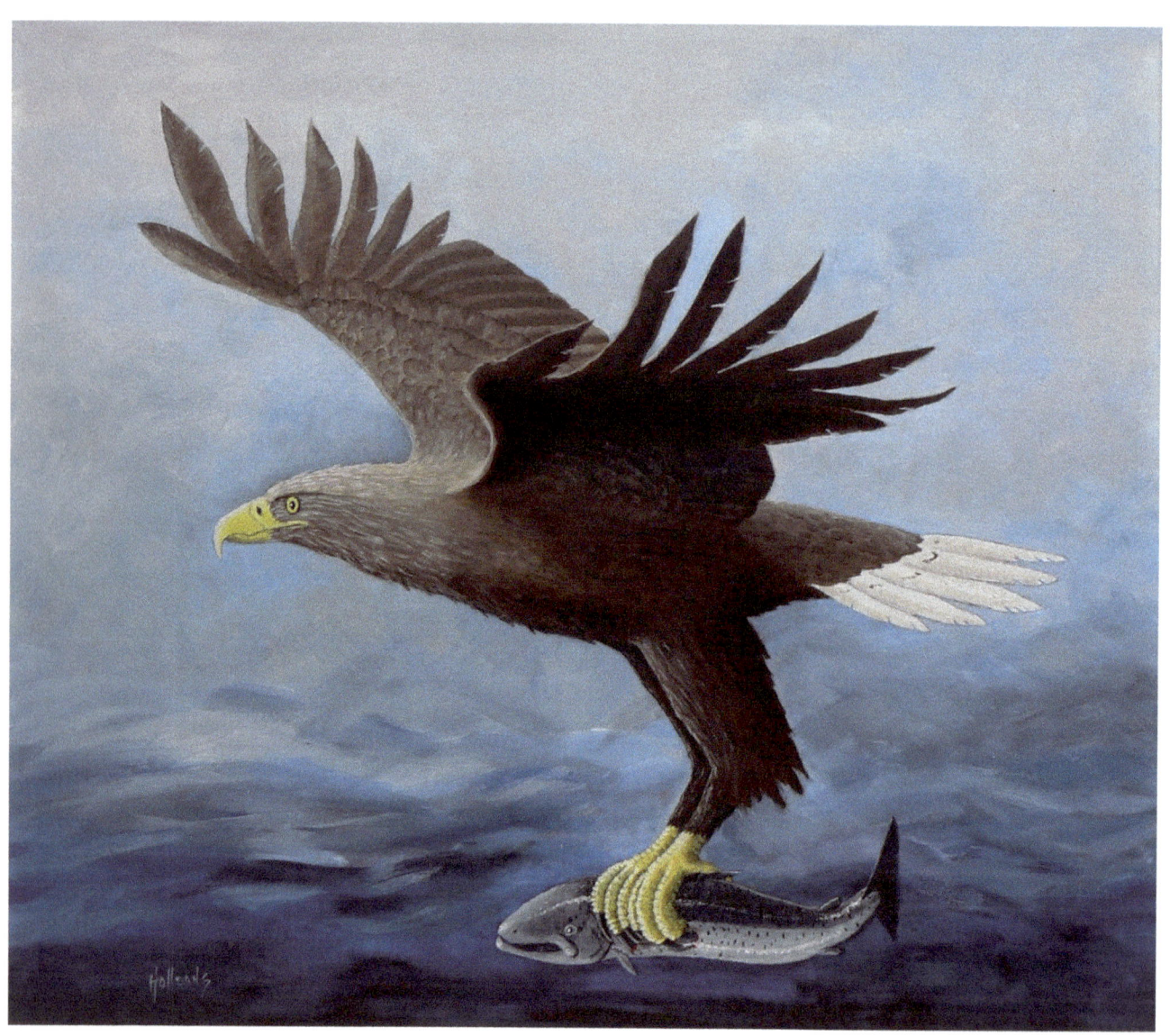

25

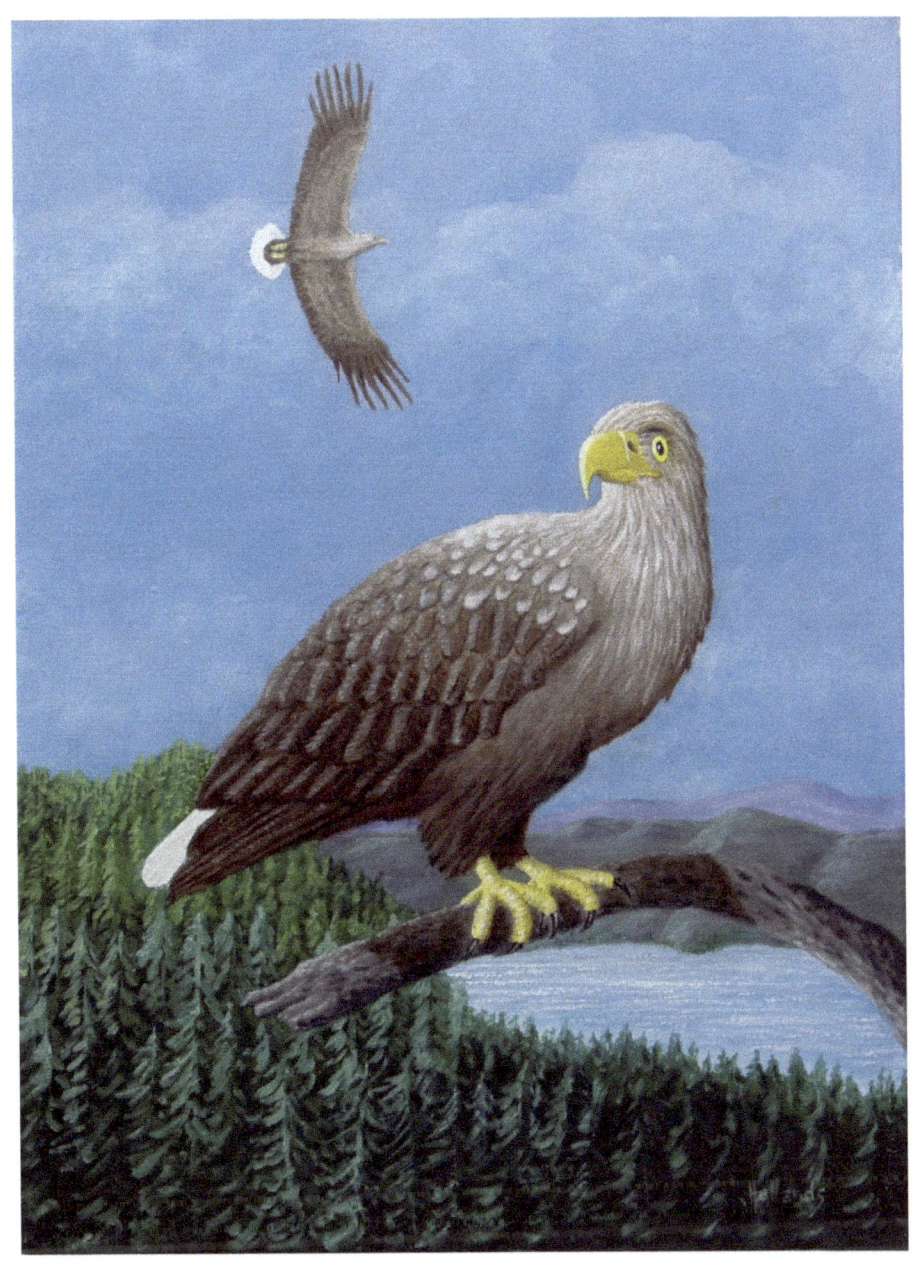

26

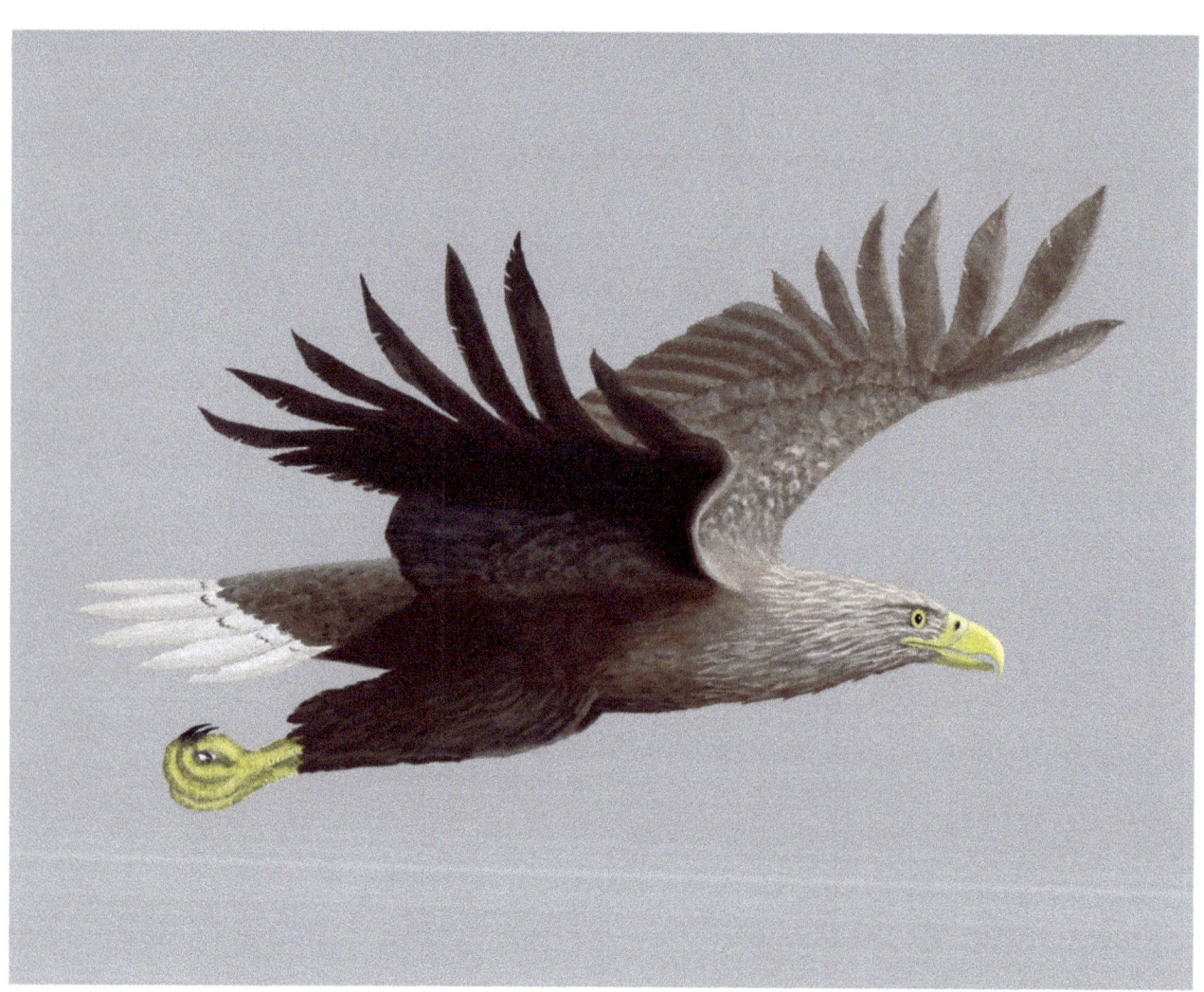

Other Books of Leonard Hollands' Art

A Passion for Bird At	*Lamorna Publications*	*2011*
Compelled to Paint	*Lamorna Publications*	*2019*
Leonard's Landscapes	*Lamorna Publications*	*2019*

Books illustrated by Leonard Hollands

Romany in the Lanes
by Phil Shelley   *Lamorna Publications 2007*

Romany on the Fells
by Phil Shelley/Leonard Hollands   *Lamorna Publications 2011*

Walks with Romany
by Bramwell Evens   *Lamorna Publications 2014*

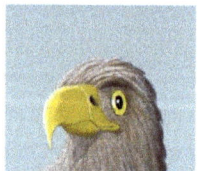

29

www.ingramcontent.com/pod-product-compliance
Lightning Source LLC
Chambersburg PA
CBHW041132280526
45792CB00013B/2388